QUEEN IN BLUE

WISCONSIN POETRY SERIES

Edited by Ronald Wallace and Sean Bishop

QUEEN
in
BLUE

Ambalila Hemsell

The University of Wisconsin Press

Publication of this book has been made possible, in part, through support from the Brittingham Trust.

The University of Wisconsin Press
728 State Street, Suite 443
Madison, Wisconsin 53706
uwpress.wisc.edu

Gray's Inn House, 127 Clerkenwell Road
London EC1R 5DB, United Kingdom
eurospanbookstore.com

Printed in the United States of America
This book may be available in a digital edition.

Library of Congress Cataloging-in-Publication Data

Names: Hemsell, Ambalila, author.
Title: Queen in blue / Ambalila Hemsell.
Other titles: Wisconsin poetry series.
Description: Madison, Wisconsin : The University of Wisconsin Press, [2020]
    | Series: Wisconsin poetry series
Identifiers: LCCN 2019039057 | ISBN 9780299326647 (paperback)
Subjects: LCGFT: Poetry.
Classification: LCC PS3608.E493 Q44 2020 | DDC 811/.6—dc23
LC record available at https://lccn.loc.gov/2019039057

For migrant mothers, and for my own

Does it see us as a couple of fireflies
    playing hide and seek in a graveyard?
Does it find us good to eat?
—**CHARLES SIMIC**

strange earth, strange
that we will die into

this bright, blue oblivion
—**ARACELIS GIRMAY**

Contents

QUEEN IN BLUE

joy

joy spreads like blood on the sheets, love, and we are black
blooded thieves, turnip takers in our lucky rabbit skins.

whiskey makes the good heart powerful and we thump thump
our drums until sunup. chant ourselves hoarse through the smoking

wet cedar. the system of currency and want has lost its sway. I have now
only the natural sorts of hunger. with that in mind, let us feast.

with that in mind, let us cleave the river from the bank with the cosmic ax.
feed the deer from our pockets, the oatmeal we ourselves were raised on

and will raise our children on again. with that in mind, ravage me.
have you seen the quiet way in fog the dawn barely breaks? it is treason

for the day to enter with so little ceremony. I want fireworks. I want
the slaughter of lambs for our holy days, but each day is holier than the last.

as we plummet from our high banyan seat the short switch beats the rug,
the golden beets are slow to come and you, love, accept my hurricane

to your stout trunk, accept the natural uprooting. the bevel meeting of me to you,
god, speak on the smoothing of stone by water, and the fitting of stone to stone.

we are meek walkers on the once lush globe. now, among the perishing, we count
our blessings and shed our shoes.

I

Son

Before you were born, you
        pushed aside the small intestine,
pushed aside the liver. You, sacred acorn,
        nestled to the sacrum.
Holy mother, holy fool, holy lunar pumpkin, I opened
        like a lion's mouth: conduit of lightning
to conduit of flood.
        Birth is a catastrophe. We go alone
to the death-gates, fetch back life.
        We alone climb the pyre, turn flame. Return
to find the story changed.

        Find in our ears the somber phonetics
of cold black stars and black ripe berries.
        Of how we carved a home here
with bone spears. Made angelic by hunger
        and colossal by love, the mountain is a small feat.
Your feet go on and on.
        To break is to be godlike, boy-child take note.
Later when you load your gun.

Mother saw the death-gates. Mother brought you back.

Passport

For the first time in your short life,
Little Egg,
   you are hungry.
You who were born
with a little blue book in your mouth
have the stomach flu
and for two days have refused even water.

   On the second night,
   hunger is haunting your room,
   wraithlike, and holding you
   I feel the spikes
   in your belly, the spongy
   ache of your gums.

But by the third day
you are ready for toast
and on the fourth day,
when you want milk,
you have milk.

I think of the Syrian boy
   I saw in the video—
You are still baby-soft

but I think
     of him anyway,
his tender skeleton
revealed—

     I have known only the outer
     edges of hunger, a fight with my father
     over unfinished milk. Food stamp milk,
     milk of lines and forms but still
     enough milk for me not to want it.

But I know this:
     How the boy's father
     holds him to his chest
     like a hole in it
     and how his mother,
     a tiger in a small cage,
     throws herself again
     and again against the wall
     of no bread.

All my dreams of war
involve children.
All my dreams
of motherhood
involve war. Birth,
a bloodbath, and then
the sudden knowing
you can kill, if you need to
you can do anything.

I imagine your skeleton.
Close my eyes, ultrasound—
giant head, perfect heart,
little penis waving around
as you somersault

in your fishbowl.

No life is easy
but
    some bones are
revealed by ultrasound
others by sonic
    boom   some
    boys watch helicopters
    fly low
    without
    dropping anything.

On the day that I made
cupcakes for your first birthday
an American gunship
bombed the hospital in Kunduz.
Today, it is the hospital in Aleppo
as I peel for you, my Goldfish, an orange.

    Someone is claiming
    this rubble is for you
    but you make friends
    everywhere we go, O
    Jubilant Ambassador,
    Open Heart Surgeon,
    Atlantic Sturgeon, O
    Call to Prayer. You, in Morocco
    kissing the ticket seller
    through the ticket booth glass,
    you on the lap of every passenger
    on every train and
    the first day back Stateside
    where you coo and flash

your gummy grin
at the women wearing hijabs
and the weird fortune
that this foreign-seeming place
is yours is lost on you.

In the mountains
that run into Mediterranean
    we drive past
those who wait
those who wait for
a boat, as we traipse
across the border
to the rattle
of a cheap rental
dance across
the border
for the stamps
that let us dance back.
These blue books
we carry worth
more than water
more than
life. They wait
in the mountains,
come to the road
to ask for water.

I don't stop.
    You
have been crying
for hours
and are finally
asleep.

My mother is trying
for citizenship still.
Reluctantly, but for you.

    At sixty-four
    she bites her tongue
    and weathers
    the years-long interrogation
    of her intention
    to share a continent
    with her grandchildren.

Meanwhile, you learn how
to say *thank you*
and I give you
an orange just to hear it.

In some villages
the three-year-olds
have lived
entirely without
flour, sugar, salt

    and the ocean isn't deep
    enough to keep them
    from appearing
    in your body.

    What their mothers
    would do to hand them
    an orange.

For you, who were born
in the sea of my blood

with a little blue book
like a hook
in your mouth

with the corned
and calloused hands
of America
steady on the reel

I would throw myself
against the wall
of war but
I can't find it.

I watch a hawk
collide with a semitruck.
It looks so inevitable.
At one and a half, you
take great pleasure in
undoing things.
Hawk, Little Hawk,
love-born and lucky,
it damn near killed me
to get you here. By
which I mean, I would
die for you, and I
almost did, but the danger
of getting you born
is the only danger

we've borne. You see?

When you try
    to say I love you
    it sounds like
    I
    you
    I
    you

    I know
    you
    get the idea.

I wished you into
this world, so
I cannot say
I didn't wish
this world upon you

    its lopsided wingbeats
    its horrors.

I show you that we
belong to each other.
I encourage your many
tiny kindnesses.
I want them to count
for something. I want you
to count something—

I lose count.

For here you are
in your quiet bed.

You wake and you sleep
to nothing
    but birds.

Spirit Gulch

Past the supine buttressed firs and muscled piñons gripping
dry soil tenderly with bird foot roots, we keep going.

My love and an old friend and me, past the beetle-eaten lodgepole
pines, hollowed of their sap but still mimicking the living.

The old friend, way back when, placed a cherry tomato
from his garden in my mouth and kissed me. We keep going.

Past the butter-and-eggs, and tracks of bighorn sheep.
He made me breakfast, something fancy, poached. Past the marmot, perched
on a stump and whistling.

We keep going through the knee-high jungle of numinous wildflowers;
indigo delphinium, Indian paintbrush in vermillion, then fuchsia, lupines
in Krishna blue. Toward the worrying thunderheads.

We drank cheap red wine out of teacups and he pinned me down on a couch.
We are out of water but
                    we keep going. I got out. We come to a hole,
lined with a quartz, a pit of crystal. At the rim, a rodent skull
picked clean.
            That was many years ago. The danger,
the weather.
            Across the valley, the peaks are streaked with iodine red;
tailings from a forgotten mine here now, forever.

What is it? What could it be, drawing all this pigment up

from the shuddering earth—

Animating Principle

Tap water elixir, opiate air,
seven thousand little feet
between me and the sea.
Calcium deposits constellate
just under the skin, discomfiting
the idea of what belongs where.

I am trying to mean something,
trying to insert myself
into this catalog of moon,
to shrink and grow un-numb
to the cycles repeating, repeating.

My anima hides her darkness
in the darkness.

Hands overflowing with river, mountains
erupting from chest, mess
of Milky Way all over, she and I recede
like the glacial sea did, stay
awake until aurora borealis
makes her southernmost show.

Last night we got stoned and
lost our hands in the gloaming.
The two of us in an empty bowl,

growing thin, then thinner,
listening for coyotes and hearing them.

History/Memory

After Raoul Peck's film I Am Not Your Negro

1

James Baldwin says *history is the present* and in the film all the brown-eyed
clean-cut white boys righteous at the lynching remind me of my father/no
my father when he was young, in the pictures I saw after his mother died.

Let me be clear. He wasn't one of those boys. His stepdad was. My Indian mother
and brother and sister all still scarred from someone supposed to be family
talking like that. We never called him anything but his name.

They kept their small house freezing, stubborn, unwinnable fight against
the gulf heat. The blinds closed the television on. My brother and sister told me
I was loved best in that house because I looked the whitest.

I didn't love that grandmother until her husband was dead and she was lost
to dementia, which made her gentle. When my brother and I visited the nursing home,
she mistook us for a couple noticed the way/tenderly, we made each other laugh.
If she had ever loved us less for being brown, she had no memory of it.

I don't believe that was the reason she was so strange to us. I don't believe she
understood my father. He rejected all she had to give him, world of white
picket fences, world that was already dying when he left for California. Then India/
fifteen years without a phone call.

Whatever love she had for us was caught up in the loss of him, her only child.
Caught up in that impossible heartbreak. Toward the end of the film,
Baldwin admits a certain reluctant fealty to America/it bursts like a wet

firecracker spinning off purple into the night hissing

in spite in spite in spite in spite in spite inspiteinspiteinspite

2

() Baldwin talks about growing up loving John Wayne but the moment
you realize that you are the Indian.

() I always thought I was the Indian/but

(ARE YOU EGYPTIAN

MIDDLE EASTERN

PERSIAN GREEK EGYPTIAN

NATIVE AMERICAN WHAT TRIBE

WHERE ARE YOU REALLY I MEAN

REALLY? YOU DON'T LOOK IT YOU LOOK

RUSSIAN FRENCH EUROPEAN ARE YOU

MOROCCAN WHERE ARE YOU FROM? I AM

ROMA AND YOU LOOK JUST LIKE MY DAUGHTER

NO

WHAT A BEAUTIFUL JEWISH WOMAN

AREYOU AFGHANI YOU LOOK LIKE THE

GIRLFROM

THE NATIONAL GEOGRAPHIC HAS

ANYONE

EVER TOLD YOU THAT)

() Does anyone ever tell you to prepare for a lifetime of cognitive dissonance?

And why not? When Baldwin says *America has no place for you,*
he's talking about the feeling that you don't belong/can't possibly belong here. It's hardly unique.

() What were my white ancestors up to during the American Civil War?
Wasn't Texas part of the Confederacy?

() When I found out they were mercenaries, I was mirthful, I mean
I laughed because it made sense. They didn't own anything.

() Sometimes you are too poor to pick a side, sometimes

you just grin, pick up your gun and gin and follow the money.

() Something very wild west about all the family apocrypha. Rumor that
my father's father's mother was half Indian and a cousin of the outlaw
Jesse James. Her husband, my great-grandfather, a sheriff.

() Nothing is ever just and nothing is ever just and nothing is ever just
and nothing is ever just and nothing is ever just and nothing is ever just
one thing or another.

3

Amid his resounding
crystal clear
assessment of America
James Baldwin
confronts
his discomfort
with his own position
among the men
whose lives
and deaths
he seeks to catalog
Medgar
Martin
Malcolm
discomfort
with having outlived them
and with the reason why
he was not
an activist but
a witness
without
discounting this
discomfort
he makes
a place in the tumble
of history for
the writer
White is just
a metaphor
for power
he says and
I know this
is correct and
I guess it's

up to the whites
(I don't know
if I am one
but I know
I can write)
to rewrite it
my son
little blonde boy
few strands of brown
shot through
might ask me some day
and what

4

    will   I   tell   him

    what

should   I tell him

    should   I tell   him

you are   the sum of you are the son

    of who you   are   you are who

    will I   tell him   you are the sum

    of   who   (?) you   are

    and what?

and   what   you   do

    next

Alaska

Whenever my grizzly stories come up, I tell the one about the mother.
Her three cubs, her three bluff charges. Asked if I was afraid I dodge,
say this is what you do: walk backwards. Speak to the bear. Show her
you are bigger than she thinks. The truth is, in those days, I did not know
how to be afraid, but some years later I too became a mother. I want the boys
to see Alaska. Denali and tundra. A bit of earth, uninterrupted. I'll teach them
to blow their whistles and sing loud. Look out for scat and no matter what
never turn and never ever run. Even the mother bear can be reasoned with.
But here I hear the news and my breath just goes. Another senseless
another childless mother another bullet. The fear knows that I am large.
I charge and charge and charge—

elegy for lilac

1

this is how something so virile, so fecund
dies so young: blushes, then bursts
thick with perfume.

just yesterday the dead were alive,
met me at daybreak. as solstice came
close, their blooms browned and crisped,
then found their way to earth, inert.

2

the cat with her quicksilver fluff
is devouring another well-fed mouse.
she leaves the bile for the flies,
doing her part for the cyclical
fattening of beasts in summer.

3

night so full of moon it might break open.
moon waiting for the breaking
to tip its fire to the grass.
grass wanting to flicker and choke
the underground city of prairie dogs.

4

this is the season of ripening,
but the dead are everywhere.
as if there is a limit. as if each
of us among the living
is pushing up against it.

Letter to the Dead

for Philando Castile

I am searching for you in the desert.
It is not a desert of dunes, nor the kind
with saguaros like awkward crucifixes or beefeaters
transformed by the brujas of Arizona.
It is the desert that lives in me, the never-ending ache
of acres of sagebrush exuding their silvery petrichor.
Clouds rushing the cavern above, arched and sea deep.

I expect to see you walking here, with bullet wounds.
I know you have chosen this place to live out
your restlessness among the scarlet blooms of claret cups
and the hawk-braving hares. Among the cryptobiota
birthing their brittle cities with nothing more than dew.
Among the deer skulls, pressed into rabbit brush,
eye sockets curtained over by brown recluse.

I love you. Do you still know that? I am trying
to hear your voice singing in the white air.
Your voice like the indigo, snow-patterned mountains
threatening the horizon, rising thunder-like
from the dust. I think I catch a note. The skin
of my lips blisters and cracks. The shadows
are not still. Flickering, they make faces,
make sounds.

Witness to a chain of bursting

balloons filled with chirping finches.
I liked to make things up in the dark, bright

yarn spider webs, name your electric
mood disease a superpower. Instead,

the nightmare of your mania:
constant smell of burning feathers,

last year's untouched dinners. A ghost
now buried in moss, now gone for days

in the snow, coked up and knocked up,
your exquisite moth chocolate eyes,

mimesis of a child who was a little prone
to trouble. I could hardly remember you.

I learned to sow the medicine, delicate,
and learned how someone doesn't die

but fragments into hydra,
rakshasa or Ophelia,

minister of mystic meth trips
down the silver-tunnels of the soul.

Sister, the day you walked out of
the labyrinth and into the kitchen

was not a day, but years of impossible
breakfasts. We used to joke about

you breaking dishes. What marvel
made apocalypse stormed through

you, what storm always in you,
what storm you
                        held.

mourning

for Charleena Lyles

after your death, I open a sweet shop
and bake dusted lemon bars and violet
macaroons every day. every day, I arrange
them into peonies in the case. every night, I polish
the silver and glass. I want a place
for you to feel enchanted and let your guard
drop. is it too late for that? you cross
an invisible train track to get there,
the neighborhood disappears in the slant
northern summer. is it too late? there are
no guns allowed in the sweet shop, but
your children have cake for free.
I make them promise to brush their teeth.
I never leave, never sleep.
my hands fold butter into dough, slice apricots,
measure in a cup, on a scale, with a knife.
I never cry in the sweet shop, never hear
the news again, just shake the cinnamon
tin over the batter and master the making:
the precious, the edible, the innocent.

the tooth

at four thirty in winter, I wake from my sleep
to witness the tooth as it busts from your gum
like a whale from the deep. you, in the teeth
with your teething, alone, aloof, the tooth like
the truth is chalky and smooth, smooth chalky
calciferous, chalk-dust, dust storm,
you wail as you should at the dull saw sawing,
dull bone drawing blood from your maw,
and I tell you the truth, gentle as I can,
that becoming human is like this. the body
is awful and betrays you, it harbors pain
in waters you thought you could trust,
the boats rust, and as your mouth becomes
a crowded room, there is nothing to soothe you,
nothing in sooth.

Jigsaw

1

Mother, you never told me how your jigsaw
skeleton was reorganized when you pushed
the golden moon of my brother's skull
through it.

And when you paced the carpet of my attic
counting the minutes between my contractions
using the wristwatch you've always had,
did you remember how long it takes
for the puzzle of bones you gave me

to break into river and
rebuild into bridge?

2

It couldn't have been the watch
with the feathers and stones.
It was much more ordinary.
But when I picture you looking at
your watch, it is always the one
from my girlhood: the gilded bird-parts,
jasper and turquoise.

3

Your deformities are twinned in me.

The willowy spine protests each bend
and lift. The hips have yet to settle
with the lopsided musculature above them.
It is the pain that tells me
how I am yours
how I am yours
                            to the bone.

4

I tell you, kids this age parrot everything
like, "It isn't working out" or "It's delicate."
You tell me a story from your childhood.

In it, all the Gujarati mothers *vousvoyer*
their toddlers so they will answer back
with the appropriate deference.

You use the French
    vousvoyer
to explain it to me.

In the story, little you learns the informal
conjugations, and stops
speaking to her two older brothers like elders.
For this, she is scolded but doesn't care.

They were your brothers and
like all children in Kenya Colony,
the three of you attended English-medium
schools anyway.

5

Over the course of this conversation,
the grudge I've held against you
for never teaching me your mother tongue
begins to budge. I try believing you
all the times you insisted
            you didn't know how
to teach us Gujarati.
For the first time, stupidly,
I hear the pain in that statement.

6

Stupid is the word that started
the whole thing because
you said it once, when I was two,
in English, and I said it right back.

7

I am raising my child in the country where I was born.
Neither you nor your mother nor my own brother
can claim this. It means something and it doesn't.

8

Your body, Mother, is the river and the bridge.
The watch and the minutes. Languages pool
in the pocket of your elbow,
underneath your tongue. Your muscles
span oceans.

And then, I see my body becoming yours.
I think of the story where Yashoda looks
inside Krishna's mouth and finds

the universe there.
I go to the mirror and
    open wide.

The Neighborhood

Akkari, Rabat, Morocco

The man with the small, sweet tomatoes
deepest red, dash of orange, dash of blue—
he liked to throw an eggplant in for the boy,
a little head of cauliflower.

Taking my hand into both of his,
    (sandstone palms, topography of decades),
he would tell me the number
of coins, of days, number of nights
in the holy month.

Nearby, the cliffs strewn with glass shards,
hovering sparks of light
and the hole that led straight down
through the roof of the cave
to sloshing, green Atlantic.

In July, at dusk, I would run
the busy road along the sea—
sun like an apricot through the smog,
smog coming in through the windows,

uninvited guest. I went about speaking
French to shopkeepers
who would anyway place their best fruit
    on my bad tongue.

II

the animals

the animals decided to rest
                          that night.

it was so quiet you could hear
                          an atomic bomb
drop
        its lovely
                    crown
of petals.

I slept so black that even the baby's cries
could not wake me. I did not know
until morning that the landscape had turned
green to orange
                          not like fall but
tang.

metaphor is no way to understand
nuclear disaster. the deer all turned white
like spirit versions of themselves. the grass
too was a ghost of itself
                          hollow leaves
crumbled to ash.

I stayed awake and waited

for death

        so sweet

            so sour

Sketching Finches

Sketching finches Darwin asks, over and over
why this yellow streak of feather, why this angled beak cathedral?
Why the pelican, penguin, or buzzard, the cocked-out stance of lizards?
See the fragile, freckled egg, the symbiosis of wasp and fig.
See the sphere turning, always toward, always away from.
You hold on. You open your mouth

to sing or pray, to breathe or moan, a gnat flies in.
Meanwhile a dance fly licks her paw, alights.
Everything is always aglow from within, exuding a secret, intangible light.
Golden, as if through a forest. The wasp eats her brother,
burrows out of the sticky fruit. The iguana makes a small incision,
sucks out the albumen. You are always striving, though

toward what you cannot say. You tell yourself it will get better. The sea keeps afloat
your island of envy and desire. The galaxy spreads around you
like a shimmering blanket of great, unknowable fleece. The water is a treacherous
body, the body is a treacherous thing, it tethers you to others, it begs
for together. The truth is, beast, your tongue is gilded.

The truth is you are no different from wolf, no different from cockroach,
no less moored to the web of breathing and dying, of hunger and survival.
     But, you give Beluga her name. You say *orchid* and *Marianas Trench*.
You write the story of your own birth, make God, and silence him.
Language is your bumblebee's wings, your gift of impossible flight.
Open your eyes. Speak.

winnowed

look how the little things
flock and school:
minnows, swallows,
herds of swallowtails

look how the tongue holds
    alabaster and *rogue*
    vellum and *vermillion*—

    vermillion! not just a color
    but the sound
    of eyes popping
    how bright
    the poppies

how loud

thank god it is april, if it is
and everything is unfurling

the nuclear apocalypse yet held
at bay

this gratitude is a feast

we will perish or evolve

or perhaps be winnowed to our smallest
most brilliant members: the ant,
the ecstatic, immortal jellyfish

Mule Poetica

I like the earth, how it lilts, tilts its head
like a grackle. How it surprises you
and how it is full of secrets. It expands
and contracts, imprudent Alice and you
never can get a handle on the size of her.

    The sky at night a window
    to the whole unknowable cosmos.
    Or a sphere that you're inside of, blue
    or thick as glue and keeping its trillion
    galaxies secret. We need a better word
    for evil. One that doesn't reek of fairy tales.

One that really addresses the ways
    we fuck with each other.
The mind won't erase, not really.
It smudges and rearranges, but remains
sovereign. We have the science.

    Still, I am dead sure
    of the weird beauty,
    planetary and human.
Splashes of blood and everywhere
the bones.
    Never mind. I think of blood
as the color red. I turn up the contrast

on my little camera phone.

    After all, I have seen how
    in boreal latitudes
    night and day are whole seasons
        and dusk can last for weeks.
    I myself am a binary, undone.

I picture a scale with evil on one side
and beauty on the other. Suddenly,
one is a vulture, the other a mushroom,
both eaters of the dead.
Then, one is a tuna, the other a shark,
quiet, efficient apparatus.
On one side is a sea cucumber,
the other a cucumber. Then they're both gone.
I see myself on both sides of the scale,
one body writhing,
    the other writing.

Young with Bad Wrists

I heard on the radio, soon our cars will not need us.
Do not worry, your favorite operating system
will be synced to the dashboard, and you
will be free to bend your neck, thumbs sending bits
soaring like shards of glitter through the cosmos.
Soon you will be soothed by the flicker even here,
in your little metal boat, while the black road
pours itself beneath you like a river.
I heard this is what we want. Oh, radio, beloved wave
technology, friend in the night, dishwashing friend,
friend while driving the endless yellow
sunflower Kansas interstate. Someone was once
uneasy with you, your low, measured voices
disembodied, the way I am uneasy with this
faith in the way forward. They say It will not
glitch like me, never decide to drive home in the buoyant
small hours, hours of warmth and abandonment.

Enough. I once loved a computer man.
A proud atheist, but one who murmured
Oh-One, Oh-One, Oh-One all night
like a monk on his knees, running fingers
over scripture, Oh-One, Oh-One.
I didn't say anything, but on my knees
in the garden, dug beets from the dirt
with my bare hands. It was summer.

I would come inside for one thing only,
his skin luminescent as a screen.
It was like dating the future,
a man who doesn't expect you to call,
won't ask you to stay. The future,
my one true heartbreak. An ache that lasts
and lasts. Young with bad wrists,
a taste of what's coming.

Oh, sweet future—
If I scroll your feed, will you feed
my soul? Will you slow
this fleeting? Will you cook
me something good?

And Then

Organ of the callous cactus,
I feel for you. Ludicrous, too-big, magenta,
cast against this dusty geology,
born only to summer. There is love,
and then there is the body.
O'Keeffe knew. No bullshit
in the landscape of sex and death.

The dirt in the desert is clean,
clear of the human
racing, as if we couldn't wait
to die. There is movement,
and then there is the tiny, unheeded swarming
of drosophila to cider,
life to drowning.

Have you ever been in a canyon so loud
with ghosts, one blew right in? I have.
A second crackle of light.
There is want, and then there is the pressing into
of coal wanting diamond.
The agony of shaping your own self into something
worth carrying around.

See there, the shapes the old sea made.
Epochs marked in ochre and rust.

There we were and there we weren't.

I tell you, there is time, and then
there is ripening to rot. The doom
of paper bag to apple. The moon,
hovering, yellow and toothy, inevitable.
Extinction is a hollow word. Blow into it.

The Wanting

Put simply, the wanting was for one thing only:
to plant a seed. To bear fruit. Never mind
the world was ending. I closed my eyes
and saw Shivashakti: Destruction himself
making love to his wife. I saw a tank gun stuffed
with daisies, the dance of nitrogen and algae.
I tended sunflowers and a few heads of cabbage,
paper machéd my fence with one-dollar bills.
On YouTube, a trembling black rhinoceros
lay on her side, dying of old age. I clipped the weeds
and warmed the cream. Whisked four yolks
with a quarter cup sugar. These were the last days
of our leisure, simple pleasure—
giving blood meal to the kitchen window tomatoes,
eating a sandwich of roast beef with horseradish.
Meanwhile, humanity waged a long war with itself,
unable to stave its great paper hunger.
At eighteen, brave and bursting, I shared a house
in Portland with two heroin junkies. They ate only ice cream
and white sugar with a spoon.
I thought they were harmless enough, but now I know.
They were killing their mothers.
It was hard to know how much longer we had.
The weather was terribly unpredictable.

I could neither numb nor fool my itching womb.

The wanting kept me spinning thread between finger and thumb,
wondering what could be sacrificed so that I might be blessed.
Tigers, I thought, I would miss, but countless others were already gone,
unnamed and unnoticed. I watched. Some eggs hatched, others were eaten.
Some kittens nursed, others lay inert. A robin careened into the greenhouse,
slumped into the geraniums. I left him there to die in peace,
but he didn't.

Think Global/Act Local

The globe is warmed/the globe is swarmed.
The guns ship in/the sons ship out. I clutch
my winning ticket my/US passport/my cupboard
of beans. My forest of pines/my Texas, Earth/
dirt road/Gulf Coast/home birth. My Indian/mother's
Nigerian midwife's steady hands. Now/again
the dirt road/again/the convent. Not the Star
of the Sea/Mombasa/where my mother learned/
Kenya/her country was not hers/and neither was heaven/
no/these are/the digital age/Sisters of Mary/Mother
of the Eucharist/funded by/the Domino's Pizza empire.

My own son this/glimmering
goldfish shimmering/goldfinch/star in a state
of constant nova/will he see/what I saw/that we knew
the lost species/only flew/so far? The nectar fields/
drifting north/each year/the monarchs/
dropping like/you know. Last time/the president
Kenyan/American/visited a vanishing
glacier/cocked his head/worried brow
gently like/a father/like a man saying/what/
what can/what can we actually do/
with our small/human lives?

I take a piece of paper/fold the corners in.
Fold them in again/And once more.

Then flip it over/invert the pockets.
Poof!/A lotus. Poof!/A fortune.

Somerset

Dandelion, O! Pearly globe
of winged germ, benighted
by your own transparency,
crushed under foal's birth
thud and splatter,
before long the pattern
galloping. Needles of pine
sweep the whole earth
with their fingers, prairie to prairie
and swoop-diving raptors ride
the heat wave blithely. The heat
waves its tendrils as if under water
and water is scarce and scarcer. The coal
mine closes the summer we summon
blacker deer tongue, blackest gall bladder.
We frighten. The arc goes wider
and wider. At no urging, a wildfire,
wildflowers, fireweed and
trillium, bucket warfare, sirens
trilling. Danger is a way of living,
a way of giving the soles of our feet
to the knife's edge, the ridge between
death and being left. We hold a babe,
hold the whole day between two palms
like a palmist. Able to locate, somehow,
a future. Bells and fiddles,

a tambourine. A two-part harmony
as the smoke sinks and settles,
waning luster of moon.
Summer sets and we learn to love
the skeletal sticks, our former forest
and the rusted sign that once read:

    Somerset, CO
Coal Mining Town since 1876

Terra Machina

Fleeing our desiccated planet
       all implosions and dust
the cool star we used to orbit
our failing gravity and insufficient gods,
I follow you into the next nebula.
Medusa of stars in violet and copper
the violence of combustion
       etcetera.
We fall a long way, descend
to a sphere turning 'round
a sun burning still.
A planet that can really hold you to it,
like a mother does.
I wander on, pressing my toes
into crumbling pitch
       black loam city
of worms, fertility, fertility,
a richness born from eons
of decay.
We know
       this place, the golden
record having landed in our forbearers'
long claws.

I pause, get lost in
       this broad web of ships, machines

humming through the night, fairy-tale-like,
spinning straw into gold. All day,
battery acid sweat
stinging exhausted circuit boards.
Field after field of servers, forever solar
panels, farm rows, titanium, cadmium, some
   elemental metallic churning—

A planet abandoned, the body unnecessary,
those who chose flesh long gone. Ecstatic,
we claim this good fortune cookie:
O Sweet Molten Center!
O Branching of Rivers!
O Blue, Blue, Blue
Sea Brimming with Toothy, Silver Bestiary!

You turn around to hear me calling.
It's a home we can make here.
We can make this work.

Unearth

I felt a little writhe: the spruce imp
    unfolding—

summer deep thunder
    in the yawning blue womb

constellations branching
    glaciers shifting heft—

suspended in the doldrums
bundled digits unweb.

The boom-bloom miniscule earthquake thud,
    right heart, left heart, spine

is a train   a track   a stacked
thimble   tower   rocking.

The body in my body is
    a body of truth   body of a spy

spangle of palladium
    fireflies.

    I feel a little writhe: meat thief pinching
    iron and salt

fistful of moon
moonless.

Then the wash
   oxytocin   endorphin   light.

Swooping crows with crowbars
   prying open bone doors—

a small red cry
a suckle-hungry mouth.

   The body falling through the body.

The other world   I have seen   you
     have seen.

III

Queen of Hearts

The Queen is beating around
her bushes, yelling to the tens and fives:
Quick! quicken the blooms, redden the forlorn
bleachy roses, their thorny teeth, their clichéd form!
The rogue hedgehogs
            tuck and roll, avoiding blush feathers
and mineral beaks, unlucky beasts
break for the bushes.

At night she unlaces
            her corset, sloughs off exhausted gowns
in hues carmine, rubicund and scarlet.
She sips a neat sip. The blackness
of the Queen's night is
            eternal moonless sea floor
            inside of mammalian heart
            a silken slick machine
the Queen is dreaming of a loon
            once heard in the Yukon

on a lake so remote
no one had ever named it.
She dreams of losing sleep

to the sound of a woman
losing her head.

The Pardoner

The king usually comes to bed after
she has fallen asleep, but on occasion
at the worst time, that is, right before
she drifts into the garden of nightshades
she planted under her
bed frame   cold frame   raised bed,
the glow-in-the-dark mushrooms, the imps
balancing *en pointe* on the petals of lilies.
When the Queen is jolted awake
by the presence of her
heart-wood   sidekick,
she tries to forgive the weight
of his body shifting the nest her own
has already made in the mattress. Regardless,
she sleeps, unlike the king, whose gear-grind
brain resists falling into the ocean of twisting
coral, light streaming through it then
dissipating entirely.

They met under one of those blossoming
trees in March, peak pink, the earth beneath
soaked and fragrant, having digested fully
the mulch of the previous year and ready to sprout
and feed again. One of them sleeps like the angel
of broken branches, just at the surface, waiting
for a snapping sound and the other has no trouble surrendering

full throttle to the rabbit hole,
falling up and up into a world that is quite different,
quite different indeed.

Eleven Ten

What nobility, what fragility, what yellowing
snail's shell, what cartoon vampire teeth,
what teething puppy with rocket ship
strapped to its back, what moon shot,
what topsy-turvy, what upside down,
what underbelly, what un-birthday, what
mercury mad haberdasher, what card
tower, what gossiping flower, what poisoned
well, what mushroom cloud, what rabbit
seen in clouds, what vision quest, what
white, what white knight, what red lip,
what red herring, what bloodlust, what lust
lust, what green money, what hero's journey,
what heroin, what tourniquet, what lost wallet,
what pocket, what pocket watch, what time is it,
what year is it, where am I, what season, what sign,
what prophesied, what augury, what tea leaf,
what I Ching, what blood cell count, what
blood pressure, what blood line, what red
line, what bread line, what depression,
what oppression, what night stick, what
traffic stop, what gunshot, what siren,
what banshee, what king, what knave,
what queen?

Queen in Blue

But today she leaves the red
petticoats, leaves the skirts
and corsets, chooses cashmere
in indigo, black jeans and boots
and climbs up through the rabbit
hole.

At the surface she first passes
the house of sweet Alice. Then,
walks through a forest of blue
spruce. The needles are so
kind, the spring of them underfoot
and all the animals naked.

She spots a great horned owl
awake in daylight and several
spotted deer.

Her head is full of lovers,
the one she kissed against
a sticky ponderosa, the ones
she only kissed but never
bedded, the one who drove
a red car with a chess board
roof and didn't even get it.

O, she wants. She wants and
wants. She fingers the undergrowth,
raspberry bushes thorny and
infinitely wilder than her own
roses, so cultivated, so restrained.
The Queen comes here to remember
youth and hunger
in solitude.

Libra Season

The Queen is taking a shower. She thinks of Shakti,
thinks of her boys. Little Jack of Roses. Ganesh
guarding the door. Shiva with his sword. The forest,
the first beast. Little gods. And how they grow.
Outside, a tree in flames. The mountains breathing
a haze of smoke, even now. Earth tilting slightly
to the left. Alice in a gingham dress, blue checks.
Checkerboard to card deck. Toppled white kings.
Shooting up in the ruins of empire. The Queen is, after all,
Queen of Hearts. She feels it all. Her heart encompasses,
compass rose, lily of the valley. Precious and deadly.
Lace of white and red over blue ink. A whale,
a spray of carrot flowers. Today, the shotgun must
be cleaned. It's rabbit stew Tuesday. Fires to the West,
Florence to the East. A thunderous applause. Indra
or Zeus or Thor. Everyone has a god for that. Everyone
has a story about human greed and a flood. The Queen
licks the blood from her blade. What we believe in
is magic. What we believe is that our children are ready.
We have taught them to look for beauty. They have learned
to unleash their tempers. They will survive
the fall.

The Gardener

She gets out of bed like
the sun, giant squid
stretching poppy-flame
tentacles down
the curved planet
and the Queen
approaches the sullen
garden once again.

Her bucket of fish
blood meal reeking, she
showers the rows,
walking meditation,
one red slippered
foot after another.

What is she mumbling
under her breath? Prayer
for the executioner, prayer
for the naïve rambler
stumbling through Wonderland
as if it were a dream.

She goes back to the shed,
puts away the bucket.
Rinses her palms, calloused

from the shovel's handle,
coils the hose and takes
her tea alone.

IV

Rome

Abalone, abalone, let me trust your slick muscle
and chambered iridescence. In the moonlight, among
the ruins, we partake of your innocence. Rome was
here. In front of this nightclub and gelato stand.
It is delicate, twinning your life to someone else's:
like balancing two fish on a scale though the fish are
still fidgeting. *I know, darling. Sometimes you want sleep,*
but the oxygen is too thick. Your blood is rich with it
and impatient as the sea. Like salted urchin before
the noble octopus, we vowed to serve each other.
Itching, we bound foot to pedal and began the work.
Over many steep days found mercy, Adriatic—
My clumsy blue wounding. Your big slow heart.

Origin Story

Strung up like a rabbit by the hind legs,
I looked you dead in the eye.
Beloved, I said, give me your ripest fruit,
give me your youth. I gave a little kick.
There is a word for you, you said, it is willful.
True, I said, bucking at the rope, twisting
my swung body stiff, then feeling the weight of it
fall. You said, I never meant a rope, and the rope
loosened. My feet back below me, I did not
light out for the mouth of the cave. Instead, I said,
I'm hungry. You cooked a big feast. There was rabbit pie,
whole fish, beef knuckle broth. There was good blood
red wine. We stayed up late. I left.

The way home was snowy and I froze my hands
catching fish beneath the ice. I thought about the rope.
Several days later, you arrived with an offering:
moonshine. I said, I never meant any of it, gesturing toward
the door. You said, I don't know what you mean. You stayed.
I did not cook anything. We went outside. It was thirty below,
the kind of cold that turns your skin to paper,
turns Andromeda bright as day. I turned back
many times.

On the day we met under an antlered skull to hunt
rabbits, the antlers remained pointing skyward

as if to say, I will not dagger you if you do not dagger
me. Neither one of us caught any more than
the other and I had no choice but to say,
You are good, and
I meant it, every word.

Glossary

I asked   you answered   with your wood-apple voice

a bayonet   a castanet   a dirge

But dear ether   with your gossamer feathers

how will I find that   in this dump-truck heap

If love is a thing   then innocent jackals

kid-gloved and lowing   taking their lovers

musty nectarines   oblivious to the dead everywhere

Just stop   I stopped you

why always with this   quizzical reaping

the philodendron's long tails   dragging

Why always this simper   umbrage and teething

I met you at vespers   should have stayed home

I tried to give you   wilderness   yellow of xanthin

smearing my mouth like   a dandelion addict

For what? Two dolls   jerking limbs in the zoetrope.

The Trouble with Sleeping

The heart moves to and fro, it comes
unstuck. It shoots, comet or cannon,
herald of imminent doom. Forgiveness is
a creeping ivy; desire, a night-bloom or nightingale,
mockingbird or chickadee, a memory.
I felt you there, in the dark, where I thought
there was a knife. The dread bird
finally come to nest. It took a heavy dose of cold
medicine to warm me to this cliff.

An aftermath of amphetamines to drop
me over. Face it, we were nightmare
in the waking world, a dream in the sack.
I dreamed it like a fool, coming back,
eating the meat. Manifest, unremitting,
beastly.

This is the song of our somnolent reunion:
Only when the needs of the body displace
the needs of every other part
is it right to return.
In a dream you can do that. You can need
just one thing.

The opium-eater knows,
what the body craves, the heart needs,

and need is like a needle. Merciless,
it sews you shut. With haste, I traded
my harvest for your organs.
I wrote of flowers opening.
Cymbals crashing. Any metaphor
to justify letting a whole field whither
for one sweet root. To justify the ruin
of an empty root cellar.

Now, my table is whole
and wholesome. And fit to burst, I lack
the mess we were. Fit to burst, I know.
It is the bones who dream
and the muscles who remember,
stronger and straighter
than the gentle kidney,
the kind, dumb heart.

For the Light

Little bombs parade the night streets,
streetlamps the gravestones of kin, light

lighting the way for light. Me, suffering
your beesting, your breathing, light

in the small hallucination of our garden,
through the window, leaking on the leeks, light,

I follow you, uncover an ecstasy of death's-head hawkmoths,
fluting, fluttering, burning their bodies up to light.

O, patient one, resister, refuser, revolver, the fire
does not go low, you don't let it, you light,

you low, on your knees before my god-parts,
my god-legs parting, you drunk at the stream,
torn at the seam of me, light—

yes, but

after so many seasons   in love with
the darkening   the one who   gets you hooked
fucks you up   sugar-sick   his
maple-dark   syrup-thick   his
two faces and   two fists   I kissed
you.

you   the sun in   late summer
up north   where   it hovers
unsetting   if I got out   without   him knowing
there you were   with a ticket
and a bottle of booze   your stick and poke tattoos
you know the way sugar moves
to the head   my lipstick   all wrong   wrong red   but
all over you   in the elevator   anyway.

yes   you would go on to break me up
inspire a long run   of break-up songs
and one-night stands   lover to lover
I went   knowing   not one of them
was you   except when it was   but

when I   left him   for you   I was
christmas lights   plugged in
little red and purple   little green   twinkling
under all that dust   I was

helium and helianthus   unburied
alive   first flight   and *since feeling is first*
that first   feeling   lives
I can tap it   like a sugar tree
proof of spiders   proof of bees
proof of stars   and proof of god
yes   God
    that queer fool
        crouched in my ribs
            having a good laugh

poem with a bat in it

this is the bat that hangs from the roof
of my mouth. bead-eyes irrelevant in a
chamber iridescent with sound. the water
drips and thus she finds the walls, then
finds the door.

> when you walk in, I am waiting
> with the bat. this is not a fantasy
> of revenge. it is about
> opening my mouth.

if it weren't for the teeth, the cave would be
anechoic. but the mouth has teeth, so,
she stays, she feeds on bugs who breed
in spit puddles, buzz about. fat and happy,
wings flapping, she waits inside my pout.
me, sucking on a chocolate.

> the bat flutters around your head,
> our cheery kitchen, my glass of red
> with fruit fly floating. she flits
> and flaps and flies back in. I close
> the door again.

Marsh Song

1

I am unkind, I am on the edge
with a woman I have seen many times, but tonight
she strikes like a match, ignites Orion's belt,
three hot stars like buttons down the front of me:
desire, desire, desire.
She is all onions, that kind of roundness, all mud
and poison oak, all Pacific storm, stunt waves and
slant rain. She brushes my arm and, listen, I know
my many selves, the ones who live quietly.
The woman laughs darkly.

2

You tell me you saw three herons like prehistoric
witches holding forth among the cattails, said you'd never seen
their cobalt underwings, their sorcery before. Meanwhile,
behind my back I twitch an itchy feather and recall
the taste of rainbow trout; the way they flip and turn until
swallowed whole. Recall the spell: candied fish skin,
flight toward beckoning moon, wildness, darkness,
thrum of spur-throated grasshoppers
chafing their legs, awake—

Hour of Unbroken Eggs

I don't know the word for this
just lightened sky, this hour
of seeing you tenderly, more
than the layers of weaknesses
and ruthlessness, layers of dailiness
will grant me when the day waxes
round and warm as stone fruit.
Call it the hour of gentleness,
hour of the hot cup,
hour when you can't help
wondering what the cranes are doing,
their bright bright white feathers,
keepers of the brackish waters,
the pair of them—
Are they sleeping?
Are they awake?
Are they mourning
in their funeral whites?
Does one of them notice this hour,
hour of light seen through an eyelid?
But I won't walk to the pond. [No.]
The cranes must have their mysteries.
Instead I let the red of day break,
open as an egg, that innocent seeming
symbol, break and vanish
into ordinary.

I'll Be Here

I caught your silhouette in profile, standing in a field
of mustard and it shook me. The wheel of an old logging
wagon, fifteen feet tall, rolled into me. I fell into Lake
Superior. Romance a failure wide as this freshwater sea
I tip into. There used to be ancient trees along this cliffside
shore. Unburied wrecks of logging ships and you in the yellow.
The dizzying scale of it all. I forsake the dreams repeating.
I make my choice, take my leave & leap. Each morning,
the body's new form. Now spotted deer, now oak-hickory.
There are things we don't choose. I'll be here, with the ghosts
of old growth. You'll be gone as well. I need a butterfly
expert. A lepidopterist. There was this little white one
who stayed on my hand, stayed on my mind, it felt like
forever.

Borrowed or Stolen, Like Children

In a glass house in Michigan, hibiscus blooms
mammoth-huge, tusk-splayed. Hot pink and impossible.

A colony of feral cats nests in the strip of woods
between my driveway and the field,

kittens born and kittens picked off. I am waiting
for the egrets to return to the marsh

but they don't. I am waiting for my mother's papers
to come, but they won't, not yet. Precariousness

as old as regret. The stakes increase.
My own child crawls into bed with me.

We watch the deer nibble the trees,
watch the rain green our view

through the aquarium window. I never knew:
was the hawk swooping for mice a sign

of plenty or of doom? Would my bad choices
ever pay off? Then again, there is power in being poor

and happy. I learned this from my mother.
You can hold it in your hands and crinkle it,

dried beehive.

You can press it, *puffball mushroom*. I am getting good at this.
You can have a home: a house, a country,

but none of it belongs to you. You just live in them and love them,
borrowed or stolen, like children, all the same.

Prayer

In a field dense with low clouds, the trees make their own light.
This weird, hot autumn: sparkle dulled by dark dust
on retreating glaciers. At the cider mill, they won't even start
the furnace. Cold cider in this cool drizzle, then,
the children in their bright rain suits. Sticky with apple juice,
they give a name to the fat, dead mouse they find lying
next to the red, Radio Flyer tricycle.
Oh, to live in their sweet, little world.

The thing is, it's the same world. It's the exact same world.
Cider mash crawling with electric yellow wasps.

Listen, every October we find a praying mantis, every October
just one. And I can't help taking it as an omen. Of what?
That we will eat the ones we love the most?
That our carnal nature is full of grace?
That strangeness is all around us, hidden, but alive? I am comforted
by her lean, green body, those sideways, alien eyes,
the odd humanity of her clasped appendages.
Her presence so close to the house can only be a blessing:
visitation from a small god, benevolent and powerless.

Some years later/after sex/you asked

what I was thinking. I was thinking: Never ask me that. But instead I said,
"The table," which had been left outside in the rain for three days by then
and was surely ruined. The day we bought the table, we had driven to Raleigh
to check out a shop called Father & Sons. It had large rooms and small rooms,
multiple floors filled with vintage Danish furniture like *Jetsons* cartoons,
racks of A-line dresses and hatbox hats our grandmothers would have saved for
or sewn themselves or thrown themselves at men for, crates of vinyl records
and comical sunglasses. I remember, especially, an actual stoplight. Our table was
blonde wood with four chairs of woven straw. We thought we could afford it.
After swiping my card, I stepped outside to answer the phone. It was my brother.
Do you remember the name of the store? I was standing under the sign when he said,
"I can't keep you on my phone plan." "Okay," I said. "We've redone our budget,"
he said, "We're having a baby!" "Oh wow," I said, "We just bought a kitchen table!"
I really did like how it looked in that house with our cheap vinyl counters, the white
paint of renters, the roaches in the silverware, the silverfish in the attic.
"It doesn't matter," I said, all those years later, meaning the ruin of our
first piece of furniture. We were still renters, but this time, a furnished place
with green walls, elm beetles and ladybugs, a swing set in the yard, a car seat
in the car, and a dark, heavy table to sit at for now, and when we leave,
to leave behind.

Night Song

You learn, slowly, to lean your coyote bones
to rest. Boy of the Dreams of Wild Animals
before I knew how the stardust would pool in your eyes,
wordless, how you would open wide the windows
to me, I knew the neon dendrites illuminating your
becoming. Now, in the fog, night gathers like an army
of ghosts. Each lamppost and mailbox a centaur or doe,
white loping dog or long-eyed horse
bending its neck to the rye, the husks. The marsh releases
its multitude of arms and you let down your guard.

Bitter mallow, bitter sweet root; brewed,
strained, consumed while Capricorn gallops
hot hooves across the cosmos. I cover you with wool,
felt stars, remember my blood was once your only sky.
I drop to my knees, listen to your breath unfold itself
like a god. I plunge my hands into the stream of it.
Surrender and surrender, sound of still water, monastery
of frogs. I start a fire from wet kindling. Cup my hands
and blow, then watch it grow.

Cusp

My body was a muscled egg, and you
the pulsing yellow

    waiting for the breaking open, the ache
    the hook and loop, the clasp
    the wake, the wick and wax, the cusp

and all around, the bellows.

    The swing, the swell, the well, the water
    the summoning spell, the yell, the shudder

of light before the dawning.

    The wait, the wash, the wailing,
    the bloom, the blood, the sailing.
    The storm, the storm, the storming.

I'll see you in the morning.

Notes

All the italicized text in "History/Memory" is written down as remembered from the film *I Am Not Your Negro*, directed by Raoul Peck.

The italicized text in "yes, but" is borrowed from an e e cummings poem.

This collection owes a debt to Lewis Carroll for the weird and twisted template of the Queen, who seems an inversion of my own well-earned rage, and whom I have attempted to humanize, untwist, and respond to.

Acknowledgments

Many thanks to Carl Phillips for selecting this book as a runner-up for the Brittingham and Felix Pollak Prizes, thus paving the way for its publication. Thanks to the University of Wisconsin Press for believing in this book.

Thanks to the Graduate Employees' Organization at the University of Michigan for making graduate school accessible to me and many others by organizing to ensure access to healthcare, childcare, and a living wage for graduate students.

Thanks to all the hard-working and dedicated childcare providers and friends who cared for my children while I wrote this book.

Thanks to the crew at Moshi Moshi for returning my sanity.

Thank you to Katie Ford and Crystal Williams for introducing me to the world(s) of contemporary poetry, and for never going easy on me.

Thanks to the Helen Zell Writers' Program for providing the time and space to develop many of these poems. I am grateful to Tung-Hui Hu and Keith Taylor for their encouragement. Thanks especially to Laura Kasischke and Tarfia Faizullah for their guidance and faith in my work.

It is an honor to count my entire MFA cohort at the University of Michigan among my friends and accomplices. To the fiction writers—Ashley Whitaker, Yasin Abdul-Muqit, Rebecca Fortes, Bryce Hayes-Pope, Samuel Jensen, Clarisse Baleja Saidi, Kristen Roupenian, and Austin Blaze—thank you for your friendship and humor. To the poets—Molly Dickinson, Austin Gorsuch, Sierra Brown, Marlin Jenkins, YoungEun Yook, Courtney Faye Taylor, Robert Heald, Tara E. Jay, and Danez Smith—your brilliance gives me so much hope, and listening to your voices helped me find my own. You are all gems.

To the sisterhood—Sandi, Laila, Jane, Brittany, and Molly—your love is the foundation of my strength.

To Dan and Emma: thank you for endless generosity and for welcoming me into your family.

To the family that made me—Mom, Dad, Rishi, and Tejas—you are the weirdest, coolest people I know. Thank you for being the fiery, strong-willed, and fiercely independent bunch that you are. I love you.

To the family I made—Sam, Shailesh, and Tariq—it's like the John Prine song. You are my everything.

I am grateful to the following journals, where some of these poems were first published.

The American Literary Review: "Rome" and "Son"
Columbia Journal: "The Wanting"
Fairy Tale Review: "Libra Season" and "Queen of Hearts"
The Florida Review Online: "Witness to a chain of bursting"
Riprap Literary Journal: "joy"
Ruminate: "Passport"
Virga: "For the Light"

WISCONSIN POETRY SERIES

Edited by Ronald Wallace and Sean Bishop

How the End First Showed (B) • D. M. Aderibigbe

New Jersey (B) • Betsy Andrews

Salt (B) • Renée Ashley

Horizon Note (B) • Robin Behn

About Crows (FP) • Craig Blais

Mrs. Dumpty (FP) • Chana Bloch

The Declarable Future (4L) • Jennifer Boyden

The Mouths of Grazing Things (B) • Jennifer Boyden

Help Is on the Way (4L) • John Brehm

No Day at the Beach • John Brehm

Sea of Faith (B) • John Brehm

Reunion (FP) • Fleda Brown

Brief Landing on the Earth's Surface (B) • Juanita Brunk

Ejo: Poems, Rwanda, 1991–1994 (FP) • Derick Burleson

Jagged with Love (B) • Susanna Childress

Almost Nothing to Be Scared Of (4L) • David Clewell

The Low End of Higher Things • David Clewell

Now We're Getting Somewhere (FP) • David Clewell

Taken Somehow by Surprise (4L) • David Clewell

Borrowed Dress (FP) • Cathy Colman

(B) = Winner of the Brittingham Prize in Poetry

(FP) = Winner of the Felix Pollak Prize in Poetry

(4L) = Winner of the Four Lakes Prize in Poetry

Acts of Contortion (B) • Anna George Meek

Bardo (B) • Suzanne Paola

Meditations on Rising and Falling (B) • Philip Pardi

Old and New Testaments (B) • Lynn Powell

Season of the Second Thought (FP) • Lynn Powell

A Path between Houses (B) • Greg Rappleye

The Book of Hulga (FP) • Rita Mae Reese

Why Can't It Be Tenderness (FP) • Michelle Brittan Rosado

Don't Explain (FP) • Betsy Sholl

House of Sparrows: New and Selected Poems (4L) • Betsy Sholl

Late Psalm • Betsy Sholl

Otherwise Unseeable (4L) • Betsy Sholl

Blood Work (FP) • Matthew Siegel

Fruit (4L) • Bruce Snider

The Year We Studied Women (FP) • Bruce Snider

Bird Skin Coat (B) • Angela Sorby

The Sleeve Waves (FP) • Angela Sorby

If the House (B) • Molly Spencer

Wait (B) • Alison Stine

Hive (B) • Christina Stoddard

The Red Virgin: A Poem of Simone Weil (B) • Stephanie Strickland

The Room Where I Was Born (B) • Brian Teare

Fragments in Us: Recent and Earlier Poems (FP) • Dennis Trudell

The Apollonia Poems (4L) • Judith Vollmer

Level Green (B) • Judith Vollmer

Reactor • Judith Vollmer

Voodoo Inverso (FP) • Mark Wagenaar

Hot Popsicles • Charles Harper Webb

Liver (FP) • Charles Harper Webb

The Blue Hour (B) • Jennifer Whitaker

Centaur (B) • Greg Wrenn

Pocket Sundial (B) • Lisa Zeidner